YOUR KNOWLEDGE HAS VALUE

Christian Mogler

Theology of TV

The impact of TV

GRIN Publishing

Bibliographic information published by the German National Library:

The German National Library lists this publication in the National Bibliography; detailed bibliographic data are available on the Internet at http://dnb.dnb.de .

Imprint:

Copyright © 2010 GRIN Verlag, Open Publishing GmbH
Print and binding: Books on Demand GmbH, Norderstedt Germany
ISBN: 978-3-640-78249-9

This book at GRIN:

http://www.grin.com/en/e-book/163111/theology-of-tv

GRIN - Your knowledge has value

Since its foundation in 1998, GRIN has specialized in publishing academic texts by students, college teachers and other academics as e-book and printed book. The website www.grin.com is an ideal platform for presenting term papers, final papers, scientific essays, dissertations and specialist books.

Visit us on the internet:

http://www.grin.com/

http://www.facebook.com/grincom

http://www.twitter.com/grin_com

Hyphenated Theology Paper

Prairie Bible College

The Theology of Television

By

Christian Mogler

Date: 25. March 2010

Outline

In the beginning stages of the early Church, two things were very prevalent: Christians' love for each other, and their community with each other. However, during the entirety of the Church's existence, those two core-values were challenged through heresies, doctrinal disagreements, and quests for power by "Satan, the prince of this world" (Eph. 2:2). Throughout time, these challenges have increased rather than decreased, and so within the last thirty years a new force emerged that competes with the growth and maturation of the Christian community: Television (TV). **1 Corinthians 6:12 says, "Everything is permissible for me, but not everything is beneficial." Watching TV is certainly permissible and can provide a great deal of fun and entertainment, but, is it beneficial to my spiritual growth?**

After analyzing and evaluating TV, I have to say that *unselective* watching of TV is contrary to the goal of *becoming more like Christ*—demonstrated in our love for God and others (discipleship)—and contributes to the trend of declining relationships in family, neighbourhood, and church (community).[1] In this paper I first want to highlight the core of discipleship within community; second, I want to analyze and evaluate TV; third, show the effects it has on us; and finally conclude and suggest a Christian response to TV.

As a **disclaimer** I want to mention three things: first, I do not assume that television is inherently evil or part of a secular-humanist conspiracy. Although many programs are morally offensive, some display clear evidence of God's grace. I believe, based on Romans 14:14, that TV, like every other object in this world, is neither good nor bad. The way it is used makes it good or bad.[2] Well used, it can be a wonderful part of our lives. But if TV is used poorly, it can be harmful.[3]

---

[1] Kevin Perrotta, *Taming the TV Habit*, (Michigan: Servant Books, 1982), 28.
[2] William L. Coleman, *Making TV Work for Your Family*, (Minneapolis: Bethany House Publishers, 1983), 15.
[3] Ibid., 13.

Second, not every person is affected by TV in the same way. Not everybody who is watching a thief will be tempted to steal as well. This is due to the fact that people come from different cultures and have different beliefs and convictions, among other things. Consequently, TV is a very nuanced subject and applies to everybody differently. In this paper I try to approach TV as objectively as possible, knowing that I will not be able to do justice to the effect TV has on every individual. Third, I am using the word TV to describe the entertainment industry such as TV-shows, movies, soaps, news, and documentaries. Since I claim that "unselective TV watching" is contrary to the goal of becoming more like Christ, I will elaborate on what I mean by unselective watching at a later point. Before I begin analyzing and evaluating TV, I want to describe the biblical goal for every Christian.

Discipleship: Jesus called us to "make disciples of all nations" (Matt. 28:19), and not merely make Christians. But what is a disciple? A disciple is a follower of Jesus Christ who sets himself apart from the world and takes up his cross to follow Jesus wholeheartedly (Mark 8:34). Here are a few characteristics of a disciple.

Faith & Obedience: A disciple is characterized by his faith and obedience to the teaching of Jesus (John 14:15). Obedient faith marks growth to maturity. It is not gained by compiling information, but by exercise: living out doctrine in choices of obedience (Phil. 3:16; Heb. 5:11-14). If in our life our faith is not reflected in action, it is dead faith (Jam. 2:17). Jesus set the perfect example: He lived a life of complete obedience to his Father even to the point of death (Phil. 3:6-8).

Fruitfulness: Jesus is the vine, we are the branches. If we abide in Him, we will produce fruit (John 15:1-8). Our job is not producing fruit; our job is to abide in Christ. If we do, the Holy

Spirit will produce, as a result of our obedience, the fruit of love, joy, peace, patience, kindness, goodness, faithfulness, gentleness and self-control (Gal. 5:22).

Love: Our lives as disciples are characterized by loving God with all our hearts, and loving our neighbor, so that they may love God with all their hearts and souls as well (Matt. 22:37-39). A disciple's love for God is reflected in their love for others (John 13:34), which proves that they are children of God and not of the devil (1 John 3:10).

Evangelism: One key aspect of a disciple is the zeal to "go to the people of all nations and make them God's disciples" (Matt. 28:18-20). We are to proclaim that "God loved the people of this world so much that he gave his only Son, so that everyone who has faith in him will have eternal life and never really die" (John 3:16).

One key aspect of being a disciple is learning the law and truth of God (Dtm. 6:7-9), so that we may *know* the truth to replace our idolatry of unbelief (Rom. 10:17), be *set free* from darkness and error (John 8:32), be *corrected* and *shown* how to live (2 Tim. 3:16), be *renewed* in our minds (Rom. 12:2), so that we may be perfect, *furnished* to every good work (2 Tim. 3:17). Discipleship needs to be done in the context of the second core of Christianity.

Community: In Genesis 2:18 we read "And the Lord God said, 'It is not good for man to be alone.'" This was true for Adam, and this is true for any living Christian: it is not good to be alone. Therefore God provided community with brothers and sisters: the church. While there is huge diversity among the people of God within the church, all are united in Christ through their baptism into the death and resurrection of Christ (Rom. 6:4). In the New Testament we read several times about the church-community. Acts 27:7 says, "On Saturday evening we gathered together for the fellowship meal." Talking about speaking in tongues, Paul says "…the whole church meets together..." (1 Cor. 14:32). The first believers "gathered frequently to pray as a group" (Acts 1:14).

The members of the church are equal and interdependent. *"For the body* does not consist of one member but of many.... The eye cannot say to the hand, 'I have no need of you,' nor again the head to the feet, 'I have no need of you.'...As it is, there are many parts, yet one body" (1 Cor. 12:12-27). Paul emphasizes the care for each other within the church when he says, "If one part suffers, every part suffers with it; if one part is honoured, every part rejoices with it" (1 Cor. 12:26). So we can conclude that the Church is a community of interdependent members with the goal of becoming more and more like Christ in love and obedience. Now let us analyze and evaluate TV and ask ourselves if and how TV contributes to this.

FACTS ABOUT TV

Occurrence? "In 1946 there were 10,000 television sets in use in America, by 1950, 10.5 million sets, by 1960, 54 million sets,[4] and nowadays 99 percent of kids ages two to 18 live in homes with a TV set. Sixty percent live with three or more TV's, and more than half have a television in their bedroom.[5] To show how important TV has become, Phil Phillips said that "even by law, television today is considered a personal necessity: New York's government signed a bill from exempting a TV set from being appropriated to satisfy money judgement."[6]

How much do we watch? The Nielson Research Institute analyzed TV usage and found that "the average household in America has the television turned on for eight hours and 11 minutes a day."[7] Eight-to-18-year-olds watch daily three hours and 51 minutes, while the

---

[4] Walt Mueller, *Youth Culture 101*, (Grand Rapdis: Zondervan, 2007), 105.
[5] Ibid., 106.
[6] Phil Phillips, *Saturday Morning Mind* Controll, (Nashville: Thomas Nelson Publishers, 1991), vii.
[7] Walt Mueller, *Youth Culture 101*, 107.

average college student watches 24.3 hours of television a week.[8] George Comstock calculated

that "teenagers, by the time they graduated from high school, would have spent more hours with

television than in the classroom—typically somewhere between 16,000 and 20,000 hours."[9] **I**

wonder if we forgot that God called us to be good stewards of our time. In the parable of

the talents in Matthew 25:14-30, the servant, who was a wise and diligent steward of the

entrusted talents, was rewarded, while the unwise servant who practised bad stewardship

was thrown out into the darkness. Ephesians 5:15-16 cautions to "be careful how you live.

Don't live like ignorant people, but like wise people. Make good use of every opportunity

you have, because these are evil days." Therefore, the question one needs to ask is, "*is*

watching TV a good use of my time?"

      EXPERIMENT: Are we TV obsessed? The Detroit Free Press did an experiment and

offered $500 to 120 families if they would stop watching television for one month. Of these, 93

said no right away. Finally, five families were selected to try the experiment. It is reported that

"Soon after they unplugged their sets, each family began to see changes in their life-styles. Some

families went to places together more than they had before. Others found themselves talking and

sharing. Parents spent more time helping their children with homework."[10] Overall, "the family

members felt more relaxed and were quicker to get their jobs done with less nagging."[11]

      Instead of what? Kevin Perotta asks an interesting question: "So here we are, spending

several years of our lives watching television. The question is: Instead of what? What else could

we be doing? Reading? Talking? Fixing the roof or playing softball or sitting on the porch?

---

[8] Walt Mueller, *Youth Culture 101*, 107.
[9] George Comstock, *Television in America*, (London: Sage Publications, 1991), 19.
[10] William L. Coleman, *Making TV Work for Your Family*, 47.
[11] Ibid..

Thinking? Praying?"[12] This question is important because the investment is so great. Comstock said, "The time that people spend on hobbies and interests outside the home declined. On the average, people spent somewhat less time in conversations and personal interactions, in leisure travel, on housework and especially gardening and animal care, on child care, and in traditional religious practice, and more time shopping."[13] As I will explore at a later point, TV isolates and takes away from social time and accelerates the process of declining relationships in family, church, and community.

Do **Christians** take television more seriously than others? Quentin Schultze observed: "Apparently not. Christians on average view the same amount of television as non-Christians; moreover, they tend to watch the same programs, except that believers tend to watch more religious broadcasts."[14] Andy Crouch made the same discovery. He said, "when I am among evangelical Christians I find that they seem to be more avidly consuming the latest offerings of commercial culture than many of my non-Christian neighbours. They are content to be just like their fellow Americans."[15] Schultze shockingly concludes that "Evangelicals´ relationship to Christ have little or no impact on their television viewing."[16]

Considering the staggering statistics, we can say that almost every household in North America adopted another very time consuming and demanding member into their family: TV. In line with that, Schultze suggests that "TV may be the Trojan horse of Western civilization. We invited it into our home—first the set, then cable and the VCR, then big-screen models with stereo and high definition. Like the wooden horse, the tube

---

[12] Kevin Perrotta, *Taming the TV Habit*, 17.
[13] George Comstock, *Television in America*, 18.
[14] Quentin Schultze, *Television – Manna from Hollywood?* (Grand Rapids: Zondervan, 1986), 12.
[15] Andy Crouch, *Culture Making*, (Illinois: IVP Books, 2008), 89.
[16] Quentin Schultze, *Television – Manna from Hollywood?* 12.

seems to benign; then its sounds and images engulf viewers, families and nations."[17] Schultze continues, "In only forty years TV has captured the time of millions of North Americans and has subverted what many people claim to stand for: strong families, moral character and democratic values."[18]

What do we watch? The Bible says in Philippians 4:8 says, "Fill your minds with those things that are good and that deserve praise: things that are true, noble, right, pure, lovely, and honourable." While there are good informative documentaries and a few good shows and movies, the majority of it is about sex, adultery, profanity, lying, cheating, stealing, disrespect for legitimate authority, racism, profane language, etc. In a study (2005) of more than 1,000 hours of programming, the Kaiser Family Foundation found that 70% of the prime-time television programs contain about five sexual incidents per hour with only 4% of these imparting information about the potential consequences of sex. This represents nearly twice as many scenes of sexual content since 1998.[19] Eight out of ten programs contain violence. In a study from 1977, Lewis figured that the average American child will see more than 11,000 TV killings by the age of thirteen, which is an average of 1,000 murderers a year.[20] A study commissioned by the president on violence in America in 1999 showed those stats changed a bit: "our children are being fed a dependable daily dose of violence, the typical American child will witness over 40,000 play murders, and 200,000 acts of violence by his 18th birthday."[21] Media publisher Mediascope discovered that,

---

[17] Quentin J. Schultze, *Redeeming Television*, (Illinois: InterVarsity Press, 1992), 179.
[18] Ibid..
[19] KFF – The Henry Kaiser Family Foundation. Article *"Number of Sex Scenes on TV Nearly Double Since 1998"* was published on 09.11.2005. Article accessed on 20.03.2010. <www.kff.org/entmedia/entmedia110905nr.cfm>
[20] Gregg Lewis, *Telegarbage*, (New York: Thomas Nelson Publishers, 1977), 45.
[21] Phil Chalmers, Video: *MUSIC to die for – Is Today's Music Killing our Teens?* (Cleveland. American Portrait Films, 2002)

Drugs and alcohol are even more prevalent than sex in the popular media. One survey found that 98% of 200 movies surveyed portrayed characters using some kind of substance. 51% of films depicted teenagers smoking, and in another 46% teenagers were shown consuming alcohol. In 3% teens were using illegal drugs with showing the consequences of it in only 13 %.[22]

TV reporter Coleen Cook realized that "They have simply discovered that debauchery sells better than virtue."[23] He said that "they were told in a set of written guidelines from a major TV news consultant that everything we produced should attempt to 'bait, lure, grab, tempt, invite, entice, arouse, beckon, seduce, attract, promise, enchant, capture, intrigue, tantalize, and fascinate.'"[24] This goes in line with Schultze when he talked about Soap operas: "Soap operas use various kinds of sexual innuendo to arouse viewers and hold their interest. They also suggest that people are locked in a sometimes fierce struggle for survival; the only way for a person to get ahead is to use sinful power – coercion, blackmail, deception, and seduction."[25] Cook summarizes by saying, "the greatest sin in TV is to be boring, and the greatest temptation is to be entertaining and interesting, even at the expense of fact, context, slant, and accuracy.[26]

Perotta raises an excellent question: "What if all the programs on television were innocuous or even, in our judgement, good? Would we be comfortable spending as much time with the medium as we do?"[27] I think TV would be not as exciting and interesting! To put it in plain words: SIN makes TV interesting. *My question is: why do we want to derive enjoyment from something God absolutely hates?* Paul Washer once powerfully said, "You go to a youth meeting and you want God to move, but before you go there you watch programs on television that God absolutely despises. And then we wonder why the Holy Spirit has not fallen on a place

---

[22] Denise Boyd, Helen Bee, *Lifespan Development*, (Toronto: Pearson, 2009), 340-341.
[23] Coleen Cook, *All that Glitters*, (Chicago: Moody Press, 1992), 75.
[24] Ibid., 76.
[25] Quentin Schultze, *Television – Manna from Hollywood?*, 4-5.
[26] Coleen Cook, *All that Glitters*, 76.
[27] Kevin Perrotta, *Taming the TV Habit*, 12.

and why you have to create false fire and false excitement."[28] If we are truly serious about "bearing fruit in every good work and growing into the full knowledge of God" (Col. 1:10), why do we—intentionally or unintentionally—feed our mind with something that is contrary to the knowledge and love of God?

Why do we watch? In a research project done in 1987, Denis McQuail offers a four-fold response for common reasons to use media,[29] which, I believe, also reflect the attempt to meet the watcher's conscious and unconscious desires. As long as desires are in line with the character and will of God, they are very legitimate. However, Quentin Schulzte recognized that "because we are inheritors of the fall, we seek immediate gratification and personal pleasure rather than the kingdom and will of God."[30] This is where it gets problematic: meeting legitimate needs and desires (like sexuality) in an illegitimate way (outside of marriage). Having said this, here the four common reasons:

Information:[31] People watch TV for general interest's sake, for self-education, to find advice for practical matters or opinions and decisions, to find out what is relevant, or just to satisfy their curiosity. The desire for education is good and even biblical. In Deuteronomy 6:6-7 we read: "Never forget these commands that I am giving you today. Teach them to your children." Education is important and in the will of God, provided that it reflects reality—something I deal with at a later point— and is glorifying and honouring to God and not man or this world.

---

[28] Youtube – Broadcast Yourself. The "*Paul Washer Project*" was done by Peacy and uploaded on 25.07.2007. Accessed on 20.03.2010. <http://www.youtube.com/watch?v=AYsClDclvf0>
[29] Prifysgol Aberystwyth University. Article "*Why do people watch Television*" was written by Daniel Chandler and first published 1995. Accessed on 13.04.2010. <http://www.aber.ac.uk/media/Documents/short/usegrat.html>
[30] Quentin J. Schultze, *Redeeming Television*, 166.
[31] Prifysgol Aberystwyth University. Article "*Why do people watch Television*".

Personal Identity:[32] People desire to find reinforcement for their personal sense of value, finding a model of behavior or to gain insight into one´s self. Talking about TV quiz programs, McQuail discovered that people watch them in order to compare and compete with the expert which makes them feel really good. The quest to find one´s identity is a desire God put in our hearts, and therefore it is of no surprise that the apostle Paul exhorts several times to find and know the identity one has in Christ (like Ephesians 1, Colossians 2). It is important to have security and confidence in who one is; if not, one experiences what Eric Erickson calls Role-confusion,[33] and is like a wave of the sea, blown and tossed by the wind (James 1:6). However, it is crucial that one finds and defines his identity in and through Christ and not in what the world teaches. Therefore, the desire is legitimate, but TV usually does not offer a biblical answer about how we can meet this desire.

Integration and Social Interaction:[34] Many people watch in order to identify with others and gain a sense of belonging, obtaining a substitute for real-life companionship due to loneliness, making up for neglect and a lack of social contacts, gaining insight into circumstances of others, enabling one to connect with family and friends, or fulfilling individual needs. As I earlier elaborated on, community and relationships are of crucial importance and very basic for humanity. Unfortunately some people are so far away from real community and intimacy experienced in relationships that they need to have this virtual community presented in TV. So once again, legitimate desire met in an illegitimate way.

---

[32] Prifysgol Aberystwyth University. Article "*Why do people watch Television*"
[33] Denise Boyd, Helen Bee, Paul Johnson, *Lifespan development- 3rd Canadian edition*, 28.
[34] Prifysgol Aberystwyth University. Article "*Why do people watch Television*"

Entertainment and amusement:[35] According to the online etymology dictionary, *muse* means "to be absorbed in thought."[36] Putting the prefix 'a' in front of the word, *amuse*, changes the meaning drastically: "to divert from serious business."[37] This means, people watch TV for amusement, to "divert from serious business," to stop thinking and pondering about life, to escape problems and reality. Other people, however, just like to relax, fill their time, and experience emotional release or sexual arousal.

Everyone experiences stress and tension and it is a legitimate desire to experience relief from it. The way TV offers to relief stress and tension is by entering a 'virtual artificial world' that helps just to forget about the stress and problems one experiences. Perrotta realized that "TV does indeed provide an easy temporary relief from the difficulties our society tends to produce, but it does not help us actually deal with the causes of our tension, social fears, loneliness, or whatever problem we may be trying to escape by viewing."[38] This echoes Neil Postman: "TV takes time away from the serious contemplation of anything. Therefore TV is distracting the public from the issues of the world."[39]

While TV promotes 'suppressing stress' as a relief, God´s Word, on the other hand, suggests another type of relief: "be still, and know that I am God" (Psa 46:10). Nowhere does scripture say that we should just shut down our mind when we are stressed, but it suggests that we should "renew our mind" (Rom. 12:2) and "not to be anxious about anything, but in everything by prayer and supplication with thanksgiving let your requests be made known to God" (Phi 4:6).

---

[35] Prifysgol Aberystwyth University. Article "*Why do people watch Television*"
[36] Online Etymology Dictionary. Accessed on 13.04.2010. <http://www.etymonline.com/index.php?term=muse>
[37] Online Etymology Dictionary. Accessed on 13.04.2010. <http://www.etymonline.com/index.php?term=amuse>
[38] Kevin Perrotta, *Taming the TV Habit*, 26.
[39] George Comstock, *Television in America*, 53.

The desire of sexual arousal, however, is not to be met through watching TV, but through the marriage partner. God´s Word is very clear on that: "But I tell you that if you look at another woman and want her, you are already unfaithful in your thoughts" (Mat. 5:28). Lust is not a legitimate desire. In Ephesians 2:2-4 Paul writes that, "all of us lived among the disobedient at one time, gratifying the cravings of our sinful nature and following its desires and thoughts," but "if you are guided by the Spirit, you won't obey your selfish desires (Galatians 5:16)."

While people watch TV to meet different legitimate and illegitimate desires, doing so also arouses and shapes our desires (At a later point I also talk about how TV can shape our worldview and behavior).

Consumerism: Nobody likes them, but they contribute 27% to the average TV playing time: commercials.[40] Postman said, "The fact of the matter is that television not only delivers programs to your home but, more important to the advertising community, it also delivers you to a sponsor."[41] Postman continues,

> In fact, the reason popular TV series get on the air and stay there is that they can deliver the right audience for a sponsor, an audience that sees commercials and buys products and ideas. Advertisers and suppliers of programs spend a fortune in ratings and surveys such as Nielsen or Arbitron, slicing, dicing, and chopping numbers that will tell them what you are watching along with every bit of information about you they can get, because the more they know about you, the easier it is to sell you something.[42]

Supporting the reality of money making through commercials, Postman estimates that in 1991 even non-profit organizations such as the ABC network made 40-50 million dollars on

---

[40] Neil Postman, Steve Powers, *How to Watch TV News*, (London: Penguin Books Ltd., 1992), 126.
[41] Ibid., 2.
[42] Ibid., 2-3.

commercials aired on the news alone.[43] Therefore Postman rightly titled one of his chapters

proactively "are you watching TV or is TV watching you"?[44]

Postman said, "There are approximately 25,000 different commercials on network

television every year. This is necessary to keep pace with the two hundred or so new items

that appear every week on drugstore and supermarket shelves across the country."[45] This

means that advertisers have to produce commercials that will be noticed and will motivate

viewers to spend money.[46] Considering that producers are willing to spend up to a million

dollar for a short commercial, shows, that their endeavours to motivate the viewer to buy

the promoted product is quiet successful.

But why? Postman answer: because they appeal to our feelings and create and

direct our desires. For example, "boredom, anxiety, loneliness, rejection, fear, envy, sloth

are reality, and the remedies for each of these and more are called Scope, Comet, Toyota,

Bufferin, Alka-Seltzer, and Budweiser."[47] AXE shower gel promotes itself that way: "The

Axe Effect may result in, but is not limited to, unrelenting female attention and/or late

nights." R.J. Lavidge pointed out that if the commercial resonated with one´s emotions, it

stimulates and directs the desire which will possibly lead to a purchase.[48] Considering the

reality of commercials, I can only endorse Dr. Michael B. Rothenberg´s complain:

> While the code of Hammurabi in 2250 B.C. made selling something to a child or
> buying something from a child without power of attorney a crime punishable by
> death, our children are exposed to some 350,000 television commercials by the time
> they reach 18.[49]

---

[43] Neil Postman, Steve Powers, *How to Watch TV News*, 6.
[44] Ibid., 1-9.
[45] Ibid., 119.
[46] Ibid..
[47] Ibid., 125.
[48] George Comstock, Steven Chaffee, *Television and Human Behavior*, (New York: Columbia University Press, 1978), 317.
[49] Gregg Lewis, *Telegarbage*, 74.

I established the fact that nearly every household has a TV and that the average North American watches several hours a day. I analyzed the content of TV and suggested four reasons or 'desires they want to meet' for why people choose to invest their precious time into TV. Considering all of this I want to tackle the question of what impact TV has on our belief and behaviour.

Worldview? A worldview is described as lens, a model, a picture, or a framework consisting of fundamental beliefs through which we view the world and our calling and future in it.[50] "Some of us consciously choose our worldviews; but more often than not, we assimilate our worldviews as unconscious and subconscious collections of information they've picked up along the way [in other words: we learn by imitation]. Much of that information comes from media."[51]

Is television really able to change adults' minds? Can it cause us to see the world anew, reject our old views, and adopt new ways of thinking and living? Perrotta says, "Not singlehandedly, but television plays an effective part in changing our minds."[52] Jerry Mander points out that one reason for this is that "most TV imagery moves at a speed faster than the human eye, which means the message comes faster than we can reason with it. Consequently, TV stops the critical mind."[53] In line with that, Walt Mueller says, "As television communicates its lessons to a passive and usually uncritical audience, it becomes, as communications theorist Comstock has said, 'an unavoidable and unremitting factor in shaping what we are and what we will be.'"[54] Cook mentions that "several years ago, when ABC introduced the first lesbian character into a new TV series, the actress who played the part

---

[50] Walt Mueller, *Youth Culture 101*, 84.
[51] Ibid..
[52] Kevin Perrotta, *Taming the TV Habit*, 85.
[53] Jerry Mander, *Four Arguments for the Elimination of Television* (New York: William Morrow, 1978), 249.
[54] Walt Mueller, *Youth Culture 101*, 105.

admitted: 'I hope to create subliminal tolerance for a lesbian character which will come from the writing and my portrayal.'"[55]

Many TV-shows reflects and cultivates the mindset of this world, which is often contrary to the mindset of God as we read in 1 Corinthians 1:18, "the word of the cross is to them that perish foolishness; but unto us who are saved it is the power of God." Perrotta continues, "The desires and feelings TV arouses are often directed toward ends which are different from the ones God has planned. The models it presents are of men and women who live without him."[56]

Perrotta cautions, "The danger of television is that while holding the correct set of beliefs about God and his Word, we are allowing something quite different to shape our minds."[57] Cook challenges and says, "Can you indulge indiscriminately in television and resist being conformed to the world it presents?"[58] Therefore television is in conflict with the Christian ideal of seeing the world.

Behaviour? Does it impact how we live? In order to answer whether or not TV has an impact on our life and lifestyle, Roderic Gorney reported about an experiment with 183 adult males, ages 20–70, in the American Journal of Psychiatry. "Participants who watched violent programs tended to be more personally aggressive and irritable. But those who viewed 'helpful' or pro-social shows for a week were more even-tempered, attentive, and helpful toward their families—as judged by their wives and measured by psychological testing."[59] Three researchers at the Unvierstiy of North Carolina's Child Development Centre revealed that "a once-a-day exposure to regular Saturday morning programs over eleven days resulted in an increase in

---

[55] Coleen Cook, *All that Glitters*, 111.
[56] Kevin Perrotta, *Taming the TV Habit*, 114.
[57] Ibid., 21.
[58] Coleen Cook, *All that Glitters*, 109.
[59] Gregg Lewis, *Telegarbage*, 137.

interpersonal aggression 200 to 300%."[60] Gregg Lewis reports that one 34 year old inmate who

had spent fifteen years of his life behind bars claimed, "TV has taught me how to steal cars, how

to break into establishments, how to go about robbing people, even how to roll a dunk."[61]

Matthew 12:34 is very applicable in this discussion: "For the mouth speaks what the

heart is full of." If one fills his mind with violent shows, his mouth or even whole body will

speak accordingly. Therefore Lewis right on when he says "no one can watch *National

Geographic* specials on some wonder of nature without being awed by the beauty and

complexity of God's incredible creation."[62] If we fill our mind with godly material, our mouth

will speak accordingly.

So the findings of researcher Rebecca Collins from the Kaiser Family Foundation are

only logical: "Teenagers who are exposed to a large amount of sexual content on television

programs are twice as likely to have sexual intercourse as teenagers who have less exposure to

such programs."[63] Perrotta adds on that, "The years of research during television's first age have

shown clearly that television heightens viewers' aggressive mood and leads to more aggressive

behaviour."[64] So we can say that television is not only shaping our worldview, it is also

impacting our behaviour. Since the content is often disobedient to God's Word, it will impact our

behaviour accordingly.

The problem: I settled that TV impacts our behavior and shapes our worldview.

Romans 12:2 calls us to "not be fashioned according to this world: but to be transformed by the

renewing of our minds." The problem is that the presented mind transforming philosophy in TV

---

[60] Gregg Lewis, *Telegarbage*, 48.
[61] Ibid., 47.
[62] Ibid., 139.
[63] KFF – Kaiser Family Foundation. Article *"Teens With More Exposure to TV Sexual Content Twice as Likely To Have Sex as Those With Less Exposure, Survey Shows"* was published on 07.09.2004. Author unknown. Accessed on 20.03.2010. <http://dailyreports.kff.org/Daily-Reports/2004/September/07/dr00025617.aspx>
[64] Kevin Perrotta, *Taming the TV Habit*, 77.

is from this world and more often than not contrary to the will and character of God. Lot of TV's content is not only evil in the sense of blunt disobedience to God's command, but is also misrepresenting reality; it is not true. In case the viewer would catch that TV distorts reality, everything would be fine. However, Lewis realized that: "Television's picture of reality is readily accepted by great numbers of viewers."[65] In other words, distorted realities (or lies) are sold as truth, and the viewers believe it and direct and shape their lives and worldview accordingly.

This means there is a "competition for truth." On one hand we have God's Word which proclaims truth and gives direction for life. On the other hand, as Mueller said, "the entertainment-industry developed the masterful ability to provide teenagers with 'compelling maps of reality' that serve to guide them through the maze of adolescence into adulthood. Media interprets and defines life for teenagers, and is, therefore, raising the next generation."[66] What does this distorted reality look like?

Reality? Lewis summarizes it very well:

TV distorts reality by presenting a simplistic picture of life. In the real world, personalities are terribly complex, motives are mixed, and some problems go unsolved forever. But television projects a world of clarity and simplicity. People demonstrate clear-cut dominant characteristics, motives are obviously plain (if they are not, the star always explains them during the epilogue), and unless the plot is to be continued next week, every show ends with all problems resolved.[67]

While with some shows, like cartoons, we know that they are not real, many shows, such as reality shows, are presented as real but are not. Phillips cautions that "Adults must realize that fantasy is not a false reality. It's a setting aside of true reality."[68] **In line with that, Postman stated that "the measuring stick for public information and entertainment in America**

---

[65] Gregg Lewis, *Telegarbage*, 88.
[66] Walt Mueller, *Youth Culture 101*, 83.
[67] Gregg Lewis, *Telegarbage*, 92.
[68] Phil Phillips, *Saturday Morning Mind* Control, 9.

today is not whether something is true, but whether it is interesting."[69] This is, because

television is simply too easy to turn off, so it must be enticing.[70] Mueller compiled quotes

about "Things Hollywood Has Taught Us." Three of them are: "It is easy to land a plane,

providing there is someone in the control tower to talk you down" and "a man will show no pain

while taking the most ferocious beating, but will wince when a woman tries to clean his

wounds," and "if you are blonde and pretty, it's possible to become a world expert on nuclear

fission, or anything else, at the age of 22." But let's take a closer look at one example:

Violence: The portrayed violence in TV is often distorted and does not show the whole

picture. As an illustration I want to use Coleman's observation:

> If there is a fight in the bar, most people seem to be enjoying it. One person gets thrown
> up against the wall; a second has a chair broken over his back, while a third is thrown off
> the balcony. Ha! Ha! Ha! One thing we often forget is that a broken nose hurts. A person
> thrown off a balcony could easily be killed. A chair broken over someone's back could
> stop him from walking straight again.[71]

So while people laugh about people getting beaten up or even killed, they do not learn from TV

what reality is: violence actually hurts and is cruel. Besides distorting reality, TV has other

effects on us. The problem is, that "studies have shown that the more violence a person sees, the

more desensitized to violence they become."[72]

EFFECTS

Morality - Right and wrong: God gave us for the majority of decisions a clear moral

standard, revealed in the Ten Commandments in Exodus 20. Based on our knowledge of them,

we shall live (Phil. 3:16; Heb. 6:11-14). While in most movies the story turns on the characters'

selection of good or evil, courage or cowardice, we think that our faculty of distinguishing right

---

[69] Coleen Cook, *All that Glitters*, (Chicago: Moody Press, 1992), 71.
[70] Coleen Cook, *All that Glitters*, (Chicago: Moody Press, 1992), 71.
[71] William L. Coleman, *Making TV Work for Your Family*, 84.
[72] Phil Chalmers, Video: *MUSIC to die for – Is Today's Music Killing our Teens?* (Cleveland. American Portrait Films, 2002)

from wrong should be exercised. This is often not the case. Instead, as Perrotta said, "television usually dulls rather than sharpens viewer´s sense of right and wrong."[73] William L. Coleman elaborates, "Conflicts in TV often blurs the difference between right and wrong. It sometimes distorts them so badly that you cannot tell which is which."[74] He continues and argues "that sometimes on TV conflict is not between good and evil but between bad and worse. Television shows 'good guys' doing evil things for a good cause which can easily lead us to think that sometimes it is OK to do bad things for a good cause."[75]

Anti-Social/Isolation: As mentioned in the first part of this paper, the call to Christian discipleship leads us together with fellow Christians. Disciples of Christ are not 'lone fighters' but 'team players.' We are "brothers and sisters" in Christ who belong to "one body." The author of Hebrews said, "Let us not give up meeting together, as some are in the habit of doing, but let us encourage one another--and all the more as you see the Day approaching" (Hebrews 10:24-25). **However, Schultze recognized that "TV is often like an enormous vacuum that sucks up people´s God-given talents by cutting them off from other people.** Having said this, Coleman recognizes that "if most of our time is spend as a hermit sitting in a room, we might have trouble getting along with people. It is a skill to get along with people and it has to be practised regularly."[76] I realize that watching TV is a comfortable thing to do. I do not need to deal with 'difficult people' or initiate a conversation. But, is the simple way always good?

One statistic shocked me: "Among the 8-18 year olds, 63% live in a home where the TV is usually on during meals."[77] Mealtimes are often the only time the family sits together and talks about how they are doing. However, if the TV is on, the focus will not be on the family but on

---

[73] Kevin Perrotta, *Taming the TV Habit*, 117.
[74] William L. Coleman, *Making TV Work for Your Family*, 87.
[75] Ibid..
[76] Ibid., 63.
[77] Walt Mueller, *Youth Culture 101*, 108.

the TV. In line with that, Perotta was right on when he said, "television's subtraction of time from relatives, friends and neighbours may make our lives easier. But ultimately it makes us poorer."[78] Watching TV has the potential of isolating people. Perotta adds on that "While our relationships with other Christians are important, television has contributed to weakening these ties."[79] Television is not the main force behind the breakdown of people's relationships, but it quickens the processes of isolation and anesthetizes us to them.[80]

Passivity: Considering that by the age of 14, the average person has seen 11,000 murders, we do not need to be surprised that injustice and violence in school and society does not really affect us any longer; 'it is just an ordinary thing.' Perotta points out that this passivity is the cause of another problem: "It distracts us from the opportunities to serve the many needy people who are around us if we would take the time to look for them."[81] In other words: contrary to our call to love and care for each other, TV makes us numb to the people around us.

Creativity? While creating a TV show or a movie demands lots of creativity, watching TV, on the other hand, does not. Watching TV is consuming the creativity of others. A good comparison is going out for food. While it certainly demands creativity and work for the chef to prepare the Cordon Bleu, it does not require any creativity or work on our side. We, the customer, just consume the finished work of the chef. (If the food is good though, it may inspire to do some own home-cooking.) There is nothing wrong with going out for supper and enjoying the creativity of others. However, if this becomes our default, we may not only become dependent on the creativity and work of others, we also miss our calling. Crouch said that "Human beings were made in God's image: just like the original

---

[78] Kevin Perrotta, *Taming the TV Habit*, 29.
[79] Ibid..
[80] Ibid..
[81] Ibid..

Creator, we are creators."[82] We are called to be creative. Creating means that just like Adam & Eve came up with names for all the animals (Genesis 2:20), we use our God-given minds and create something new, such as a meal, song or artifact. Watching TV, however, makes us to passive speculators and consumers and, therefore, undercut our potential and deprives us from our privilege to be active creators. We rob ourselves and do not even know it.

Fear: How many of us have experienced having a night-mare based on a movie we watched the night before? Coleman said that "some studies suggest that if we watch many frightening shows on television, we become afraid. "[83] He elaborates, "If we watch too many robbers, fights or murders, we start to imagine things. We become more afraid of the dark than we need to be. We think that something will happen when we are perfectly safe."[84] Dorothy Singer reported that "Sesame street researchers surveyed 233 children ages six to eleven of diverse backgrounds. Nearly two-thirds of the children indicate intense anxieties about guns, death, and violence. The fear engendered by television or film can last for many years."[85]

I can concur with that. At the age of 15 or so I watched the Thriller "Seven" and the movie scenes were haunting me for years after. Many fears we have, for example that somebody will jump out of the bush with and threaten or kidnap me, are caused by movies we watched. Singer said, that "even fictional stories of violence and danger vividly presented on television can create distressing emotions that may recur periodically for years."[86] Additionally, George

---

[82] Andy Crouch, *Culture Making*, 23.
[83] William L. Coleman, *Making TV Work for Your Family*, 35.
[84] Ibid..
[85] Dorothy G. Singer, Jerome L. Singer, *Imagination and Play in the Electronic Age*, (London: Harvard University Press, 2005), 70.
[86] Ibid., 85.

Gerbner's found in his research (1986) that, "those who view more television have an outlook different from those who view less, and see the world as more mean and risky."[87]

To the glory of God? Throughout the ages, it has always been God's purpose to bring glory to Himself (Ex. 8:22; Ezek. 39:7; Col. 1:27), because "he is jealous for [His] holy name" (Ezek. 39:25b). Satan was kicked out of heaven and became the "god of this world" (2 Cor. 4:4) because he was jealous; he wanted to be like God, he wanted to have God's glory. Talking about Satan, Isaiah 14:12-14 says, "I will raise my throne above the stars of God; I will sit enthroned on the mount of assembly." The way Satan tempted Adam and Eve into sin was the same pattern: "If you eat from this fruit, *just as God*, you will see what you have done, and you will know the difference between right and wrong" (Genesis 3:5; italics mine). Ever since our temptation has been to 'be like God' and receive glory and honor. Ever since, the glory that is due to God has been embattled.

In Quentin Schultze's book *Television, Manna from Hollywood*, published in 1986, the author said that he "discovered that most Christians genuinely desire to use television in God-glorifying ways, but they sense that the task is too complicated to undertake alone."[88] Therefore he suggests that "the Church is the best place for concerned Christians to begin discussing how to use media constructively."[89] My question is, *do we still care to use television in God-glorifying ways?* **To me it seems more probable that Christians accept the 'badness of TV' and uncritically indulge in it, regardless of where the glory goes.**

However, since God is the Creator and Saviour, he is worthy of all glory and honor. Because of that, Paul writes to the church of Colosse that, "whatever you say or do should be done in the name of the Lord Jesus, as you give thanks to God the Father because of

---

[87] George Comstock, *Television in America*, 117.
[88] Quentin Schultze, *Television – Manna from Hollywood?* 134.
[89] Ibid., 135.

him" (Colossians 3:17). One possible interpretation of this is that the chief purpose of a Christian is to bring glory to God. Though it may sound harsh, but there are only two receiving ends of the glory: God, or not God; there is no in-between. Having said all of this, here is my question: *"is the TV content we watch glorifying and honoring God's character and commandments? If it is not God that is glorified, who is?*

SO WHAT?

After analyzing and evaluating the content of TV, I have to conclude that most of the content we are entertained by is not of great help in our quest to build community and discipleship -- being drawn closer in love and relationship to God and others. But what can we do? I concur with Postman who says, "While we can't do much about the rapid growth of new technology, it is possible for us to learn how to control our own uses of technology."[90] But how can we control it? As Schultze recognized, "there is no major movement afoot, even among Christians, to renounce television or offer any alternatives to it."[91] In line with St. Augustine I would agree that "complete abstinence is easier than perfect moderation."[92] Therefore my personal preference and maybe simplest solution would be "no TV – period."

However, not everything on TV is 'evil' and 'contrary to the will of God.' It can be used for our edification and God's glorification. Therefore, besides checking for content, what are good questions to evaluate our TV habits?

Do I watch too much? When we know how to quote Bart Simpson or 'The Office' but do not know how to quote the Word of God, we may have set the wrong priorities and meditated longer on the TV-control than on the Word of God. Perrotts asks, "When is there time to lift our

---

[90] PBS- Online Forum. Interview with Neil Postman was done on January 17, 1996. Page accessed on 20.03.2010. <http://www.pbs.org/newshour/forum/january96/postman_1-17.html>
[91] Quentin Schultze, *Television – Manna from Hollywood?* (132.
[92] Quotationsbooks. Publishing date of quote is unknown. Author of quote is St. Augustine. Accessed on 20.03.2010. <http://quotationsbook.com/quote/112/>

minds and hearts to God? When are there quiet moments in our busy coming-and going days to read scripture, to ponder its meaning and refresh ourselves with reading a spiritual book?"[93] (Please find "The TV is my Shepherd" in the attachment). *Maybe this is the time to do a TV fast.* Do you remember the experiment? A question worth asking ourselves is: *Could I live one month without TV?* If we want to be good stewards of our time, we need to acknowledge that with every hour we spend in front of the TV we lose valuable time to invest in growing closer to God and others. With every hour we watch TV we miss out on serving the last, lost and the least. **Therefore, Schultze suggests asking this fundamental question: *"Is this what God would have me do with my time and talent?"*[94]**

Selectiveness: Dr. Paul Borgman stated that "our family´s most deeply shared experiences have been viewing certain family shows together, at times both children and parents even have cried."[95] Talking about family shows, such as 'Little House on the Prairie,' he continued, "shows that portray the realistic, complex, emotional problems of everyday living can inspire the most worthwhile improvements."[96] Therefore it is important not to over-generalize TV.

There are good and educational or pro-social TV-shows, such as the 'Discovery Channel' or 'Extreme Makeover: House Edition.' Watching sport events, such as the Olympic or the World Cup, can have positive effects on a national scale. There are also excellent movies, such as *The Passion of Christ*, *Luther*, and *10 Commandments*. Documentaries about various subjects of this world and human history are often very informative and God honouring. Therefore, condemning TV as a whole would be like

[93] Kevin Perrotta, *Taming the TV Habit*, 27.
[94] Quentin J. Schultze, *Redeeming Television*, 168.
[95] Paul Borgman, *TV – friend or foe*, (Illinois: David C. Cook Publishing Co., 1979), 62.
[96] Ibid., 65.

throwing out the baby with the bathwater. Therefore, as mentioned in the introduction, the keyword is selectiveness.

However, Schulzte is right when he said: "We all joke about how bad television is, but we still watch it."[97] Therefore he suggest that "**rather than choosing the easy way and criticize the television industry we need to get our own viewing in order.**"[98] Therefore, as people do **not just eat any food that lies around—rotten or not—we should not just watch anything that is on TV. Why? As rotten food makes us sick, so does 'rotten TV.'** While there are **different criteria we apply in evaluating whether or not the food is eatable, so should we also evaluate the 'TV-food' we eat. Let us get critical about what we feed our minds with.**

Evaluation: **One suggestion is to create our own "TV evaluation." To do that, I adapted from Ted Baerh some practical evaluating questions:**

What is the premise of the movie? Does the premise agree with, or conflict with, biblical truth? How is the premise solved? How are God and his word portrayed? What are the moral statements? What does it say about violence, sexuality, lying? Who is the hero? Who is the villain? How are religion, Christians, and the Church portrayed? How is the world portrayed? How is reality portrayed? How is evil portrayed? How is government portrayed? How is love portrayed? How is family portrayed?[99]

The TV guide or online movie-reviews can be of great help to answer those questions.

Another aspect of evaluating the content of TV is to reflect on it and talk with others about what we liked or disliked. This way we do not just uncritically consume but evaluate the content of whatever we watch. As we talk about what we watch, our discernment may increase and we may realize it may be better to not watch this type of movie or show in the future. Additionally it helps us get to know the people we are watching with and may actually build community. Without conversation and reflection, it is just consuming a "product."

---

[97] Quentin Schultze, *Television – Manna from Hollywood?,* 8.
[98] Quentin J. Schultze, *Redeeming Television,* 166.
[99] Ted Baerh, *The Movie&Video Guide for Christian Families,* (Nashville: Thomas Nelson Publishers, 1987), 28-42.

Schultze said, "Discriminating viewing requires us to see programs for what they really are in the light of the gospel, not in the shadow of our own tastes and desires."[100] Therefore, in the next step, one should compare the answers the movie or show suggested with what the Word of God says.

Having 1 Corinthians 6:12 in mind, which says that "everything is permissible for me, but not everything is beneficial," after evaluating the 'TV-food' with the suggested questions, reminding ourselves to run the race—being a disciple—that is set before us (Heb 12:1), and exercising maturity by discerning between good and evil (Heb. 5:14), we now need to decide whether or not we eat the 'TV-food.' One caution I have to give: if TV substitutes community and church-life, even the most God-honouring TV-show like Bible-TV becomes contrary to God's purpose and will for our life.

WWJD? In line with that, here another thought: For a period of time it was "in" to ask "What Would Jesus Do?" We can still ask this question: "Would Jesus watch this movie?" If we first check out what this movie is about, and realize that its content is anything but God-honouring, we can assume that Jesus would not watch this film. Would Jesus derive enjoyment from watching people "acting" how they bluntly disobey their father and indulge in adultery, divorce, stealing, killing, etc.? I mean, we do not know for sure, but I doubt it strongly – at least not for entertainment. However, I can see Jesus watching a movie for the sake of reaching out to somebody, or to talk about the movie afterward. Indeed, I have heard a few good movie-sermons! The same concept, but put in another question is: **"Would you be embarrassed to sit through the movie with your parents, your children, or Jesus."**[101] **Baerh continues and**

---

[100] Quentin J. Schultze, *Redeeming Television*, 166.
[101] Ted Baerh, *The Movie&Video Guide for Christian Families*, 42.

says, "When we are alone, we often deceive ourselves regarding the true nature of motion

picture [TV]."

<u>Motif?</u> Perrotta cautions us as well to examine *why* we are watching TV. He said,

> Are we trying to escape difficulties in our relationships with the people we live with?
> Are our children having problems in school or with friends that are causing them to
> withdraw to the comfort of the screens? Are there frustrations in our jobs which are
> causing us distress? Do our schedules not allow us time for better kinds of
> recreations?[102]

If any of those questions are answered with yes, one is running away from reality and it is

highly recommended to face the problems or situation.

<u>Alternatives?</u> Lewis stated, "prevention is not good enough. We need alternatives and

good replacements."[103] Considering the current state of TV, Crouch would say we can condemn

TV;[104] critique it;[105] copy and adapt to it;[106] or consume it.[107] While uncritical consumption is

however, none of these will really help us to build relationships and create an atmosphere of trust

and love. Crouch said "the only way to change culture is to create more of it; we will have to

create something new.[108]" In line with that, the only way we can change the current state of TV

is by creating something new. There have been many attempts to copy and adapt to it (movies

like *Passion of the Christ*; *Luther*) and were quite successful. However, in order counter the

impact TV is having on our Christian society through its often God-denying and dishonouring

content is through creating something new, an alternative.

One good way to find "alternatives" is by looking back and thinking about what we, or

people before us, did before TV was as popular as it is nowadays. I remember that in our family

---

[102] Kevin Perrotta, *Taming the TV Habit*, 139.
[103] Gregg Lewis, *Telegarbage*, 135-136.
[104] Andy Crouch, *Culture Making*, 84.
[105] Ibid., 86.
[106] Ibid., 87.
[107] Ibid., 90.
[108] Ibid., 67.

we played lots of board games or spent lots of time working outside, playing sports, helping neighbours, etc. If we truly start thinking about ways in which we can be more communal and growth-oriented, I am convinced that God will reveal to us a multitude of ways to do so.

In concluding, without demonizing TV I have to say that after analyzing and evaluating the content of television, unselective watching of TV may be permissible, but for sure not beneficial. It is *not* fostering growth to a deeper love for God and others. Instead, due to its ungodly message, it is actually promoting a worldly mindset which will eventually show itself in our behaviour again. TV has the potential to isolate, makes us passive and deprives us from using our minds creatively to use the time in a more communal way. Therefore, if we are truly serious about growing in our knowledge of God, we may have to rethink our TV-habits and be more critical with what we –intentionally or unintentionally- fill our minds, and possibly start seeking activities that are more fostering growth in love and community.

Appendix

"The TV is my shepherd"

The TV is my shepherd. My spiritual growth shall want. It makes me to sit down and do nothing for His name's sake, because it requires all my spare time. It keeps me from doing my duty as a Christian because it presented so many good shows I must see.

It restores my knowledge of the things of the world and keeps me from the study of God's Word. It leads me in the paths of failing to attend the evening church services and doing nothing for the Kingdom of God.
Yet, though I shall live to be hundred, I shall keep viewing my TV as long as it will work, for it is my closest friend. Its sounds and its pictures they comfort me.

It presents entertainment before me and keeps me from doing important things with my family. It fills my head with ideas which differ from those in the Word of God.
Surely no good thing will come of my life because of so many wasted hours, and I shall dwell in my remorse and regrets forever.[109]

---

[109] Gregg Lewis, *Telegarbage*, 149-150.

Bibliography
Books

Baerh, Ted. *The Movie&Video Guide for Christian Families.* Nashville: Thomas Nelson Publishers, 1987.

Borgman, Paul. *TV – friend or foe.* Illinois: David C. Cook Publishing Co., 1979.

Boyd, Denise, Helen Bee, Paul Johnson. *Lifespan development- 3rd Canadian edition.* Toronto: Pearson Education Canada, 2006.

Coleman, William L. *Making TV Work for Your Family.* Minneapolis: Bethany House Publishers, 1983.

Cook, Coleen. *All that Glitters.* Chicago: Moody Press, 1992.

Comstock, George, Steven Chaffee. *Television and Human Behavior.* New York: Columbia University Press, 1978.

Comstock, George. *Television in America.* London: Sage Publications, 1991.

Crouch, Andy. *Culture Making – Recovering our Creative Calling.* Illinois: InterVarsity Press, 2008.

Lewis, Gregg. *Telegarbage.* New York: Thomas Nelson Publishers, 1977.

Mander, Jerry. *Four Arguments for the Elimination of Television.* New York: William Morrow, 1978.

Mueller, Walt. *Youth Culture 101.* Grand Rapids: Zondervan, 2007.

Perrotta, Kevin. *Taming the TV Habit.* Michigan: Servant Books, 1982.

Phillips, Phil. *Saturday Morning Mind Control.* Nashville: Thomas Nelson Publishers, 1991.

Postman, Neil, Steve Powers. *How to Watch TV News.* London: Penguin Books Ltd., 1992.

Schultze, Quentin. *Redeeming Television.* Illinois: InterVarsity Press, 1992.

Schultze, Quentin. *Television – Manna from Hollywood?.* Grand Rapids: Zondervan, 1986.

Singer, Dorothy G.; Jerome L. Singer. *Imagination and Play in the Electronic Age.* London: Harvard University Press, 2005.

Internet

KFF – The Henry Kaiser Family Foundation. Article *"Number of Sex Scenes on TV Nearly Double Since 1998"* was published on 09.11.2005. Article accessed on 20.03.2010. <www.kff.org/entmedia/entmedia110905nr.cfm>

KFF – Kaiser Family Foundation. Article *"Teens With More Exposure to TV Sexual Content Twice as Likely To Have Sex as Those With Less Exposure, Survey Shows"* was published on 07.09.2004. Author unknown. Accessed on 20.03.2010. <http://dailyreports.kff.org/Daily-Reports/2004/September/07/dr00025617.aspx>

Online Etymology Dictionary. Accessed on 13.04.2010. <http://www.etymonline.com/index.php?term=muse>

Quotationsbook. Publishing date of quote is unknown. Author of quote is St. Augustine. Accessed on 20.03.2010. <http://quotationsbook.com/quote/112/>

PBS- Online Forum. Interview with Neil Postman was done on January 17, 1996. Page accessed on 20.03.2010. <http://www.pbs.org/newshour/forum/january96/postman_1-17.html>

Prifysgol Aberystwyth University. Article *"Why do people watch Television"* was written by Daniel Chandler and first published 1995. Accessed on 13.04.2010. <http://www.aber.ac.uk/media/Documents/short/usegrat.html>

Youtube – Broadcast Yourself. The *"Paul Washer Project"* was done by Peacy and uploaded on 25.07.2007. Accessed on 20.03.2010. <http://www.youtube.com/watch?v=AYsClDclvf0>

Video

Chalmers, Phil. Video: *MUSIC to die for – Is Today's Music Killing our Teens?*. Cleveland. American Portrait Films, 2002.